BOOK SOLD
NO LONGER R.H P.L.
PROPERTY

Mission: Space Science

Journeys to Outer Space

Megan Kopp

Mission: Space Science

Author: Megan Kopp

Editors: Sarah Eason, Tim Cooke, Ellen Rodger

Editorial director: Kathy Middleton

Design: Paul Myerscough and Lynne Lennon

Cover design: Paul Myerscough

Photo research: Rachel Blount

Proofreader and indexer: Nancy Dickmann, Wendy Scavuzzo

Production coordinator and prepress technician: Ken Wright

Print coordinator: Katherine Berti

Consultant: David Hawksett

Produced for Crabtree Publishing by Calcium Creative

Photo Credits:
t=Top, tr=Top Right, tl=Top Left

Inside: Flickr: NASA Johnson: p. 42; NASA: pp. 7, 10, 14, 15, 20, 21, 23, 24, 25, 26, 28, 30, 31, 37, 41; NASA, ESA, and D. Coe, J. Anderson, and R. van der Marel (STScI): p. 18; NASA, ESA, G. Dubner (IAFE, CONICET-University of Buenos Aires) et al.; A. Loll et al.; T. Temim et al.; F. Seward et al.; VLA/NRAO/AUI/NSF; Chandra/CXC; Spitzer/JPL-Caltech; XMM-Newton/ESA; and Hubble/STScI: p. 11; NASA/GSFC: p. 40; NASA/Goddard Space Flight Center/Conceptual Image Lab: p. 39; NASA Goddard/Chris Meaney: p. 36; NASA/JPL-Caltech: pp. 5, 12, 16, 17, 19, 33, 35, 45; NASA/WMAP Science Team: p. 22; NASA/JPL-Caltech/Malin Space Science Systems: pp. 13, 32; NASA/JPL-Caltech/University of Arizona; Figures 1 and 2: NASA/JPL/UA/Lockheed Martin: p. 44; NASA/JPL-Caltech/University of Arizona/STScI; Figure 3: NASA/STScI/AURA; Animation: NASA/JPL-Caltech/University of Arizona/STScI: p. 38; Shutterstock: Freestyle Images: pp. 1, 34; Anton Jankovoy: p. 6; Liquid Studios: p. 9; Paulista: p. 8; Sdecoret: p. 27; Triff: p. 4; Wikimedia Commons: Jeff Foust: p. 43.

Cover: Shutterstock: NASA Voyager Spacecraft illustration

Library and Archives Canada Cataloguing in Publication

Kopp, Megan, author
    Journeys to outer space / Megan Kopp.

(Mission: space science)
Includes index.
Issued in print and electronic formats.
ISBN 978-0-7787-5393-3 (hardcover).--
ISBN 978-0-7787-5404-6 (softcover).--
ISBN 978-1-4271-2208-7 (HTML)

    1. Manned space flight--Juvenile literature.
 2. Outer space--Exploration--Juvenile literature. I. Title.

TL793.K644 2019   j629.45   C2018-906106-5
                                                      C2018-906107-3

Library of Congress Cataloging-in-Publication Data

Names: Kopp, Megan, author.
Title: Journeys to outer space / Megan Kopp.
Description: New York, New York : Crabtree Publishing, [2019] | Series: Mission: Space science | Includes index.
Identifiers: LCCN 2018050348 (print) |
  LCCN 2018051460 (ebook) |
  ISBN 9781427122087 (Electronic) |
  ISBN 9780778753933 (hardcover) |
  ISBN 9780778754046 (pbk.)
Subjects: LCSH: Manned space flight--Juvenile literature. | Outer space--Exploration--Juvenile literature.
Classification: LCC TL793 (ebook) |
  LCC TL793 .K65484 2019 (print) | DDC 629.45--dc23
LC record available at https://lccn.loc.gov/2018050348

Crabtree Publishing Company

www.crabtreebooks.com   1-800-387-7650

Printed in the U.S.A./032019/CG20190118

Copyright © **2019 CRABTREE PUBLISHING COMPANY.** All rights reserved. No part of this publication may be reproduced, stored in a retrieval system or be transmitted in any form or by any means, electronic, mechanical, photocopying, recording, or otherwise, without the prior written permission of Crabtree Publishing Company. In Canada: We acknowledge the financial support of the Government of Canada through the Canada Book Fund for our publishing activities.

Published in Canada
Crabtree Publishing
616 Welland Ave.
St. Catharines, Ontario
L2M 5V6

Published in the United States
Crabtree Publishing
PMB 59051
350 Fifth Avenue, 59th Floor
New York, New York 10118

Published in the United Kingdom
Crabtree Publishing
Maritime House
Basin Road North, Hove
BN41 1WR

Published in Australia
Crabtree Publishing
Unit 3 – 5
Currumbin Court
Capalaba QLD 4157

Contents

CHAPTER 1
What Is Outer Space? 4

CHAPTER 2
How Do We Explore Outer Space? 8

CHAPTER 3
Deep Exploration 16

CHAPTER 4
Humans in Outer Space? 24

CHAPTER 5
Ship Shape 30

CHAPTER 6
What's Next? 36

ACTIVITY
Your Space Science Mission 44

Glossary 46
Learning More 47
Index and About the Author 48

CHAPTER 1
What Is Outer Space?

Outer space begins about 60 miles (100 km) above the surface of Earth. Humans cannot live there. There is not enough air to breathe. Stars shine in blackness above the atmosphere because there is no air to scatter light and make the sky blue. The distances between objects in space are so big that they are not measured in the units of length we use on Earth. Distances in outer space are measured in **light-years**.

Distance and Light

A light-year is the distance that light can travel in one year. Light travels at a specific speed of about 186,000 miles (300,000 km) per second. Doing the math, this means that light travels around 5.9 trillion miles (9.5 trillion km) in a year. The nearest star to Earth is 4.3 light-years away. The distances into deep space measure into the billions of light-years.

atmosphere

Outer space begins at the edge of the atmosphere, which is the envelope of gases that surrounds Earth.

Stars and their solar systems group together in space in massive clusters known as galaxies.

Defining Space

Space is full of stars, **planets**, **asteroids**, and **comets**. These features are all clumped together in **galaxies**. Our **Solar System** includes the Sun and the planets that surround it. It lies on one of the spiral arms of a galaxy called the Milky Way, one of 100 to 200 billion galaxies that exist in the universe. The closest galaxy to ours is the Andromeda Galaxy. It is 2.3 million light-years away.

Telescopes are used to help scientists see into space. They can see as far as 13.7 billion light-years. What lies beyond is a mystery. Our universe may not be the only one that exists. No one really knows how big space is. It is possible that space is much, much bigger than we think it is today.

Future Finds

Our understanding of space comes from scientific research and **theories**. As we continue to dig deep into the unknown, we find new pieces of information that constantly change, challenge, and confirm our current body of knowledge. The science of outer space is continually **evolving**. Come join the journey!

Why Explore Outer Space?

Humans have always explored. We want to know what lies beyond the horizon. In 1492, exploration took Christopher Columbus on a journey across the sea to land in a continent that no one in Europe knew existed. It took **astronauts**, or space travelers, to stand on the Moon and look back at Earth in 1969. The drive to explore will push boundaries ever further when it takes astronauts to Mars, possibly by 2030.

What Is Out There?

Space scientists are curious by nature. They want to seek out and explain the unknown. The more they learn, the more they realize how much they still do not know. Exploration raises new questions. It opens new doors and invites us in to a new level of discovery. Space exploration helps us better understand not only our own planet and Solar System, but also how we fit in the universe. It helps answer questions such as how life began on Earth, how our Solar System formed, and what forces created our universe. The benefits of exploring outer space extend beyond one nation to many countries, working together with a shared focus and goal.

> The urge to explore space is inspired by the desire to discover not only what lies out among the stars, but also what it tells us about ourselves.

Outer space is full of mysteries, such as **dark matter**, which is an invisible form of matter that acts a little like a scaffold to hold the universe together. Space mysteries are now being unraveled through exploration. In 2017, scientists found seven large **exoplanets**, or planets outside our Solar System. They were circling a red star named Trappist-1. It is the first time so many planets have been found circling one star.

Using Knowledge

Exploring outer space means developing new technology that also helps us on Earth. Tools designed to detect damage in space rockets do the same thing for bridges and buildings. Materials designed to protect against extreme temperatures in space have been used in insoles for mountaineers and distance runners in hot climates. **Biotechnology** was used for purifying water in space. The same technology has been adopted on Earth to clean large bodies of water in city lagoons and to treat waste for livestock farms. These technologies create new industries and provide new solutions to old problems.

A rocket carries a telescope into space, where it will orbit Earth as it studies the stars.

YOUR MISSION

Trappist-1 is 39 light-years from Earth. Astronomers have never seen anything like the dim star with its seven, Earth-sized planets. Each one of these planets may be capable of supporting life. Why do you think this discovery is so significant to humankind?

CHAPTER 2

How Do We Explore Outer Space?

It takes about three days to travel from Earth to the Moon. It is a mere 238,855 miles (384,400 km) or 1.25 light-seconds away. A light-second is how far light travels in 1 second. It took 253 days for the Mars Science Laboratory to reach Mars in 2012. Mars and Earth are constantly moving, but they sometimes come as close as 33.9 million miles (54.6 million km). That means Mars is about 3 light-minutes from Earth. Distances in outer space are so huge they are measured in light-years. How do scientists begin to explore such vast distances?

Mighty Big Telescopes

Astronomers use a variety of telescopes around the world to explore other stars and galaxies. These telescopes are often built on top of mountains. There is less light pollution in high, remote locations, so observations of the night sky are not distorted by the lights from cities. **Optical** telescopes, which study visible light from space, also suffer distortion caused by the atmosphere. The movement of air causes the stars to twinkle. The higher a telescope is, the thinner the atmosphere around it, so there is less distortion.

Radio telescopes detect radio waves that constantly hit Earth from objects in space.

8

The mountains of Hawaii, in the Pacific Ocean, are home to a number of telescopes.

Other telescopes study invisible radio waves. The 1,000-foot (305-m) radio dish near Arecibo, Puerto Rico, was once the world's largest single-**aperture** telescope. It uses a large dish to reflect radio signals to the receivers. In 2016, China's Five-hundred-meter Aperture Spherical Telescope (FAST) took the title. It is the size of 30 football fields.

The clear air of deserts provides ideal conditions for telescopes. In Chile's Atacama Desert, dozens of radio **antennae** make up the Atacama Large Millimeter Array (ALMA). This radio telescope array studies the processes of star and planet formation and looks back billions of years to the origin of our universe.

In the Works

The Large Synoptic Survey Telescope (LSST) is based in Chile. This optical telescope has a 28-foot (8.5-m) hole which captures light. It will image each region of the sky 1,000 times over 10 years. By 2021, when fully operational, the LSST will provide astronomers with the best-ever view of how faint objects in outer space change over time.

U.S. astronomers are planning to build the Thirty Meter Telescope (TMT) in Hawaii in the 2020s. It is a new class of extremely large telescope. It will allow scientists to see deeper into space more clearly than ever before. TMT will have nine times more area than the largest existing optical telescope.

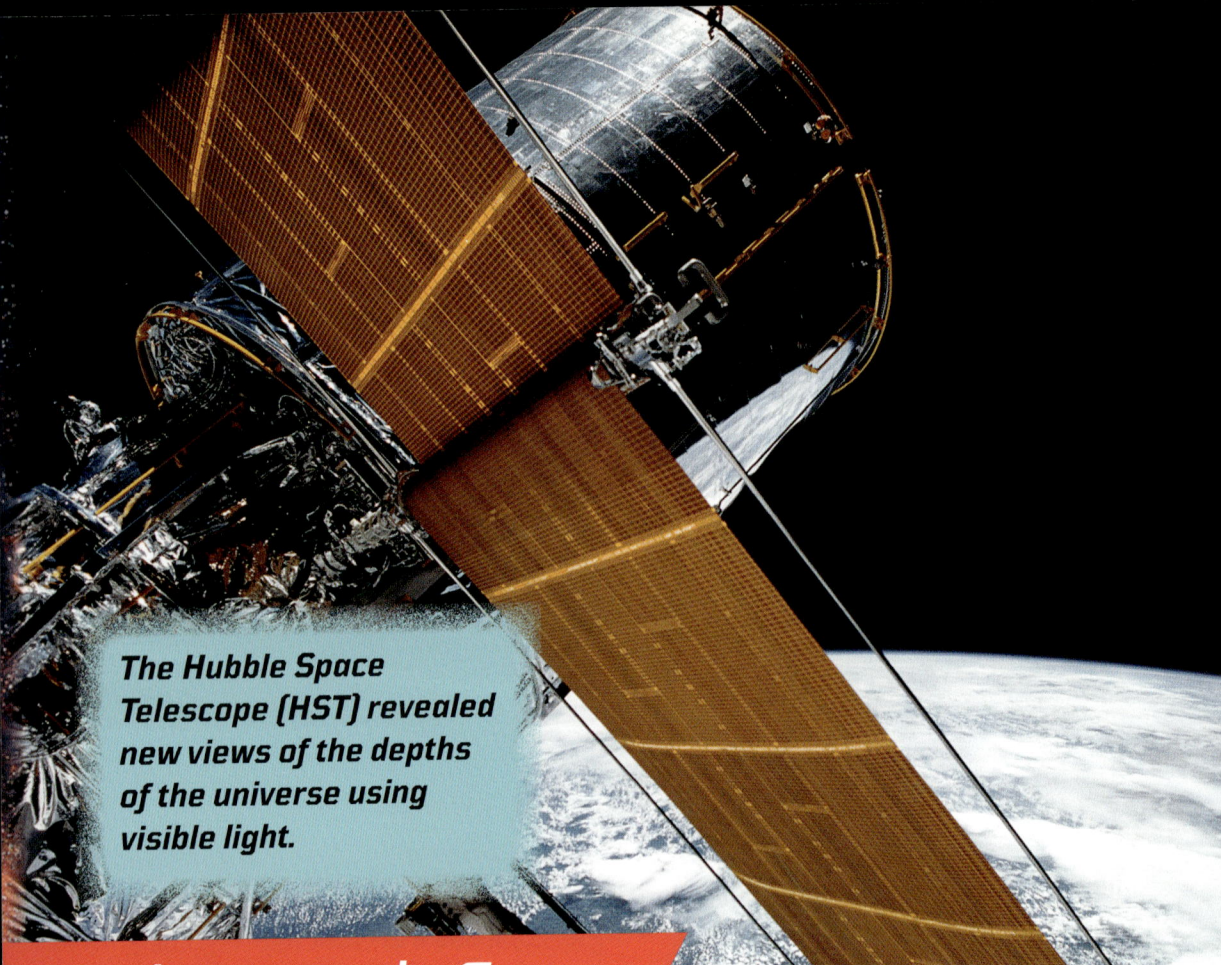

The Hubble Space Telescope (HST) revealed new views of the depths of the universe using visible light.

Telescopes in Space

Space telescopes are **satellites** that normally orbit Earth. They are more expensive to build and more difficult to maintain than ground-based telescopes. However, telescopes work better in space. Even **observatories** located in high places on Earth are affected by atmospheric distortion that limits the sharpness and clarity of images taken from Earth. This problem is solved by placing an observatory in orbit above the atmosphere.

Space-Based Study

Between 1990 and 2003, the National Aeronautics and Space Agency (NASA) launched the HST, Compton Gamma Ray Observatory, Chandra X-ray Observatory, and Spitzer Space Telescope. Each studies a particular type of light, such as visible light or **X-rays** or **infrared**, which are invisible forms of light. Compton and Chandra studied shorter light waves, while Spitzer studies longer waves.

End of the Mission

The Kepler space telescope launched in 2009. It has used visible and infrared wavelengths of light to search for Earth-sized planets in our galaxy. Kepler has discovered more than 2,500 exoplanets. In October 2018, Kepler ran out of fuel and was retired. It continues to travel through space, around 94 million miles (151 million km) from Earth, but it no longer collects data.

Once NASA realized that Kepler's fuel was running low, it made it a priority to download the recent data it had collected. To send data, the spacecraft pointed its large antenna toward Earth and communicated via the Deep Space Network (DSN). This is NASA's international system of giant radio antennae that support interplanetary space missions. All of Kepler's data was successfully retrieved before it ran out of fuel.

MISSION: Space Science

When Kepler ran out of fuel in 2018, it became a piece of **space junk**—human-made objects drifting in space. There are so many pieces of junk in space that NASA is testing methods of removing **debris**, or scattered trash. These methods will use uncrewed spacecraft that carry spearlike harpoons and nets. The spacecraft will collect pieces of debris and push them into "graveyard" orbits where they cannot harm orbiting satellites.

The aftermath of a star explosion is shown in this image. It was created using information from five space and ground telescopes.

Probing the Cosmos

A space **probe** is a spacecraft that travels to outer space to collect data. Probes use telescopes, cameras, and other equipment to gather data. Probes do not carry astronauts. Sputnik 1 was the first probe in space, in 1957. It studied Earth from orbit. Mariner 2 was the first probe to study another planet—Venus—in 1962. Today, the different types of probes are **orbiters**, **flybys**, **landers**, and **rovers**. Orbiters circle a planet or moon, while flybys pass nearby. Landers land on the surface of a space object, while rovers are designed to travel over the surface.

A 10-Year Mission

In 2017, the probe Dawn celebrated 10 years in space. Dawn's mission is to help figure out what shaped our Solar System. It is the only spacecraft to have orbited two bodies in the **asteroid belt**. This area with many space rocks lies between the orbits of Mars and Jupiter. Dawn orbited Vesta and Ceres. Vesta is an asteroid, while Ceres is a **dwarf planet**. Studying these two bodies will provide scientists with new knowledge of how our Solar System first formed and how it became what it is today.

Dawn approaches Ceres. The probe captures sunlight with its sails, and uses it to generate electricity.

Dawn has a range of tools for scientific research. It carries cameras to take images of the planet's surface, and devices to measure **gravity** on the space bodies. Tools called **spectrometers** analyze the make-up of the rocks. Dawn found that Vesta is more closely related to Earth than typical asteroids. Like Earth, Vesta has a **dense**, or tightly packed, **core**, or center. This is surrounded by a **mantle**, or middle layer, and a crust. It has a mountain more than twice the height of Mount Everest and a canyon that rivals the size of Arizona's Grand Canyon.

Exploring Mars

Mars is a main target for probe surveys. The Mars Global Surveyor went into orbit and started mapping the Martian surface in 1997. Researchers are also using rovers to explore Mars. The Spirit and Opportunity rovers landed there in 2014. The rovers surveyed the environment and took samples of soil and minerals. One goal was to survey whether the planet could support life.

The rover Curiosity took 55 separate photographs of itself on Mars. The images were combined to create this selfie.

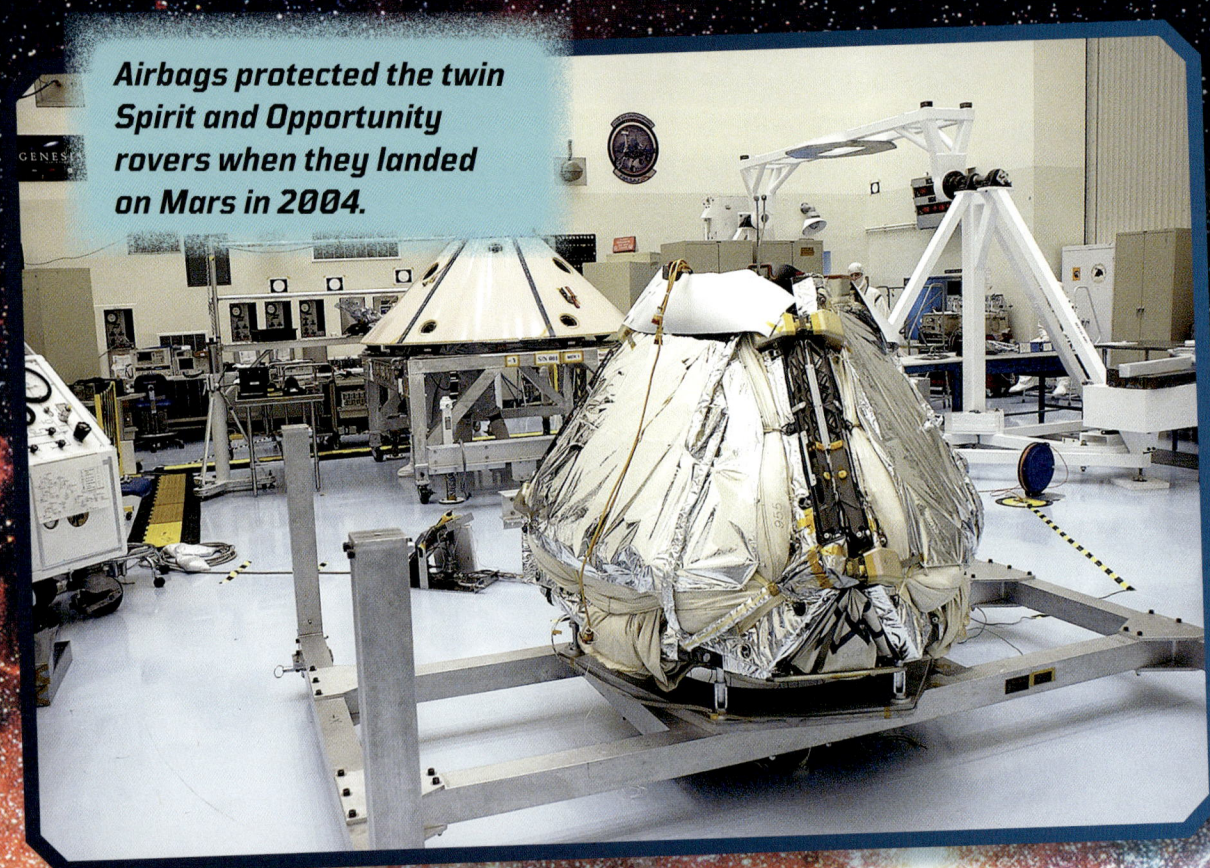

Airbags protected the twin Spirit and Opportunity rovers when they landed on Mars in 2004.

Robotic Exploration

Wolfgang Fink is a scientist who believes that **robotic** probes are the future of space exploration. Fink and his team members at Caltech, the U.S. **Geological** Survey, and the University of Arizona, are developing software that will allow robots to work in space either independently or as part of a team. These probes will be higher-level thinkers. They will be able to determine areas of interest without instructions from Earth and decide which areas they should explore first. Currently, these kinds of decisions are made by engineers on Earth who **remotely** command a rover or spacecraft to complete assigned tasks. There is little room for quick changes in their actions if something goes wrong. If Fink and his team are right, these new-age robots would be able to react almost immediately to any situation.

Into Outer Space

Robots already increase our ability to explore space. They collect data for analysis by scientists and provide a map for possible human travel in the future. Fink's **prototype** robot is equipped with a computer, batteries, and motors. There is a camera and a **sensor** that uses a **laser** to tell the rover what is in front of it. It is able to move around or back away from obstacles, and climb small rises and inclines. Fink's team is designing a system that would give the robotic rover the ability to be curious. The rover would decide where and what to explore. A laser range finder will even allow it to select a moving target and keep track of it while it follows the target around.

In the bigger picture, rovers could be designed as watercraft to explore liquid environments. Multiple robotic land and lake rovers could be overseen by air rovers in a blimp or balloon, hovering overhead to organize their efforts. New environments will be explored thoroughly, giving insight into previously unknown areas.

Robonaut 2 is a robot crew member on the International Space Station (ISS).

YOUR MISSION

Artificial intelligence (AI) is the ability of robots to learn and think like humans. Will it help space research if robots can make decisions for themselves? Explain your reasoning.

CHAPTER 3
Deep Exploration

In summer 1965, scientists realized it would be possible for a spacecraft launched in the late 1970s to visit all four giant outer planets. These are Jupiter, Saturn, Uranus, and Neptune. A rare planetary alignment would allow the gravity of each planet to help swing the spacecraft on to the next. In the summer of 1977, NASA launched two probes, both named Voyager.

Going, Going, Gone!
Voyager 1 made its closest approach to Jupiter less than two years later. The probe discovered that Jupiter has lightning and that there are active volcanoes on Jupiter's moon, Io. Neither of these **phenomena** had ever been witnessed outside of Earth before. Among other things, scientists investigated a feature known as Jupiter's Great Red Spot. They learned that it is actually a massive storm.

In 1980, Voyager 1 discovered three new moons circling Saturn. It also showed that Saturn's largest moon, Titan, has a thick, nitrogen-rich atmosphere. From Saturn, Voyager 1 began its journey out of our Solar System.

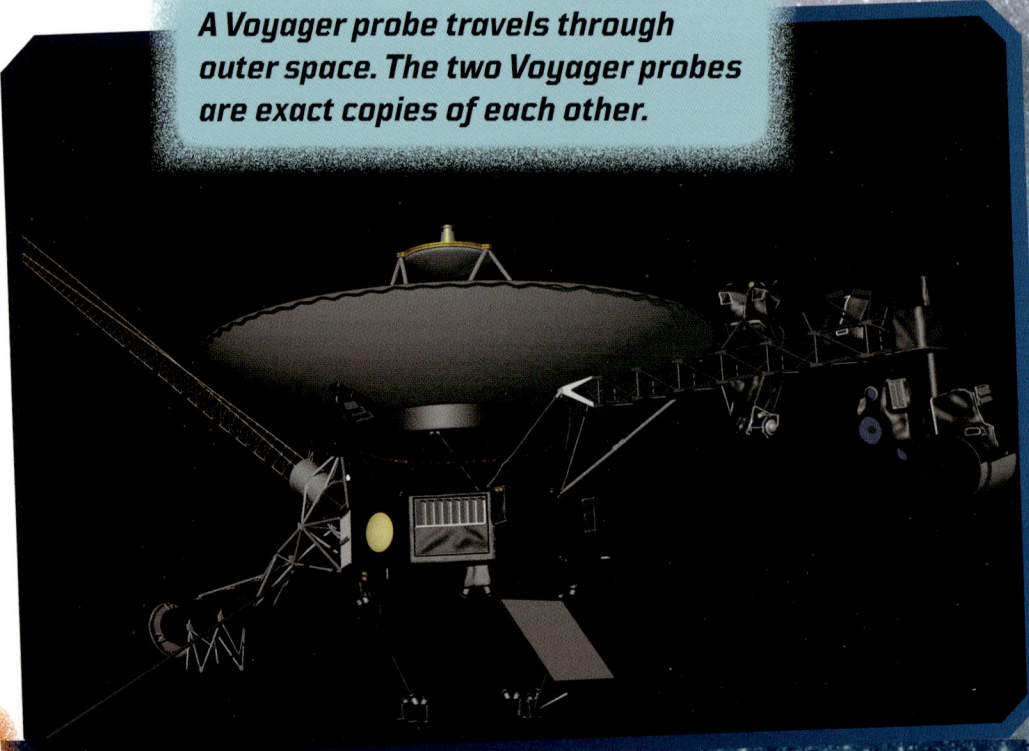

A Voyager probe travels through outer space. The two Voyager probes are exact copies of each other.

Separate Paths

Voyager 2 followed its twin, making additional discoveries at Jupiter and Saturn. It was the first spacecraft to see Uranus up close when it flew by in 1986. Among other discoveries, the probe recorded 11 new moons and detected temperatures on Uranus as low as −353 °Fahrenheit (−214 °C). Three years later, the spacecraft approached Neptune, and became the first probe to explore four planets outside of Earth. Voyager 2's photographs revealed for the first time that Neptune has rings.

On February 14, 1990, Voyager 1 took one final photo before its cameras were permanently shut down to save power and computer memory. The image is a one-of-a-kind "family portrait." It shows Venus, Earth, Jupiter, Saturn, Uranus, and Neptune all circling the Sun. As of 2018, Voyager 1 was the only human-made object to leave our Solar System and enter **interstellar space**, or the space that lies between stars. According to scientists, interstellar space begins where the Sun stops having any effect on its surroundings. Voyager 2 continued to make its way toward interstellar space.

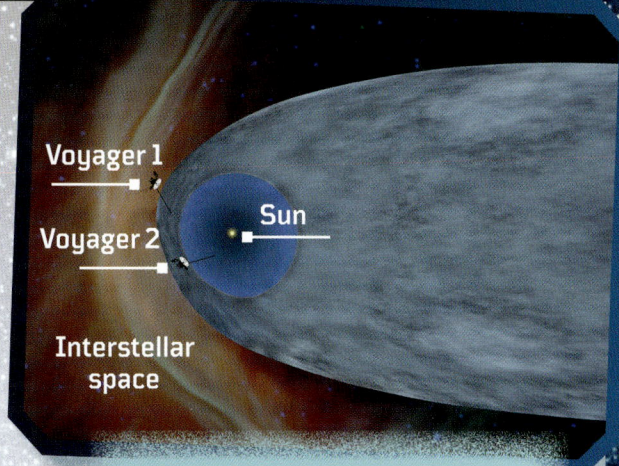

This illustration shows Voyager 1 (top) heading into interstellar space and Voyager 2 not far behind.

MISSION: Space Science

In 2017, after Voyager 1 had been gathering space dust for 37 years, its **attitude control thrusters** wore out. These small devices are vital. They turn the spacecraft so that its antennae can send radio signals to Earth. Scientists researched the technology used on the probe and ran tests on Earth to figure out how to solve the problem. They then sent commands for Voyager 1 to fire its backup thrusters. The backup thrusters have now taken over the job of orienting the spacecraft.

Dark Science

A **black hole** is a place in space that has such a strong gravitational pull that not even light can escape it. In 1916, scientist Karl Schwarzschild used the work of Albert Einstein to investigate black holes. Schwarzchild's work paved the way for the discovery of the first black hole about 50 years later. Black holes are caused by giant stars collapsing into themselves. Although we know what black holes are and that they exist throughout space, we know very little else about them. For scientists, black holes are a puzzle waiting to be solved.

larger. Our galaxy, the Milky Way, potentially has several hundred million of these hungry dark bodies.

While there may be many stellar black holes, it is the supermassive black holes that hold the power. These black holes are thought to lie at the center of every galaxy, including our own. Scientists do not know exactly how supermassive black holes form, but they may be a result of many stellar black holes merging or a group of stars all collapsing at the same time.

Different Black Holes

The three types of black holes are called **stellar**, **intermediate**, and **supermassive**. Stellar black holes are usually 10 to more than 25 times the **mass** of our Sun. Supermassive black holes are millions of times more massive than the Sun. Intermediate black holes lie in the middle. Stellar black holes are the smallest black holes, but they have a remarkably strong pull. They pull in dust and gas from the galaxy around them and grow

No one has ever seen a black hole, but in theory they appear as holes in space.

This illustration shows a black hole blowing out a column of gas.

MISSION:
Space Science

In 2018, a team of Japanese astronomers used observations from two telescopes in space and two on Earth to zero in on a flickering, supermassive black hole. Named J1354, the black hole was 900 million light-years from Earth. The scientists discovered that the black hole was "belching," or rather, blowing out huge bubbles of hot, bright gas.

Learning More

In 2015, the Laser Interferometer Gravitational-Wave Observatory (LIGO) detected **gravitational waves** for the first time. Gravitational waves are ripples in the fabric of space and time. **Astrophysicists** are interested in gravitational waves because they could help them learn more about black holes. Gravitational waves can be caused by the **merger**, or joining, of black holes. By searching for gravitational waves, scientists may discover when and how black holes joined together.

> Chandra's focus is the equivalent of reading a newspaper 0.5 miles (805 m) away.

X-Ray Vision

Looking into outer space is like looking into the past. We see distant stars as they appeared millions or billions of years ago, when the signals we see left them. In 1999, NASA launched Chandra, its X-ray observatory. Chandra observes X-rays from high-energy, high-temperature regions of the universe, such as the remains of exploded stars.

X-ray Telescopes

These high temperatures are found in many places, such as black holes. Objects at such high temperatures release most of their energy as X-rays, which are detected by Chandra's mirrors. The mirrors look like nested glass barrels. They are the largest and smoothest mirrors ever constructed.

If the surface of Earth were as smooth as Chandra's mirrors, the tallest mountains would be just 6 feet (1.8 m) high. Chandra's mirrors focus X-rays to record data. The data is reconstructed into visual images.

In 2017, Chandra took the deepest X-ray image ever obtained. It gave astronomers the best look yet at growth of black holes soon after the **Big Bang**. The Big Bang is one explanation for how the universe began. Scientists believe the universe began 13.8 billion years ago and has been **expanding**, or getting larger, ever since. Looking back at black holes that were created near the start of the universe requires very advanced tools.

Seeing Double

When astronomers using LIGO found a rare supermassive black hole pair in October of 2017, they were excited. Single supermassive black holes exist all around the universe, but double supermassive black holes are difficult to find. This was the first to be detected. To find more pairs of merging supermassive black holes, astronomers are combining data from several different telescopes that detect different wavelengths of light, including Chandra. Chandra's X-ray vision is able to look through the clouds of gas and dust that might hide black hole pairs.

Growing supermassive black holes give off strong X-rays. Chandra's sharp focus made it the perfect choice for pinpointing giant black hole pairs. More new discoveries of these pairs could help astronomers better understand the growth of giant black holes and how and why they merge. They might also lead to a better understanding of how these black holes produce some of the strongest gravitational wave signals in the universe.

Bright stars surround the supermassive black hole at the center of the Milky Way in this Chandra image.

Into the Darkness

Outer space is full of mysteries such as **dark energy** and dark matter. Such phenomena cannot be sensed, but scientists believe they exist. They hope telescopes will confirm their belief.

Ordinary matter makes up everything we see, feel, and smell, from this book to the chair you are sitting in to the smell of cooking in the kitchen. This matter also makes up the planets and stars in the night sky. It reflects light.

Missing Matter

Ordinary matter is made up of **atoms**. Everything made up of ordinary matter pulls on everything else as a result of the force of gravity. But the numbers do not add up. There is more gravitational pull in the universe than there is matter. Scientists calculate that ordinary matter makes up less than 5 percent of the universe. They believe that around another 25 percent of the universe is dark matter. This dark matter does not reflect light—instead, it bends it.

Astronomers believe dark energy might be like a smooth, unchanging surface that is more powerful than the force of gravity.

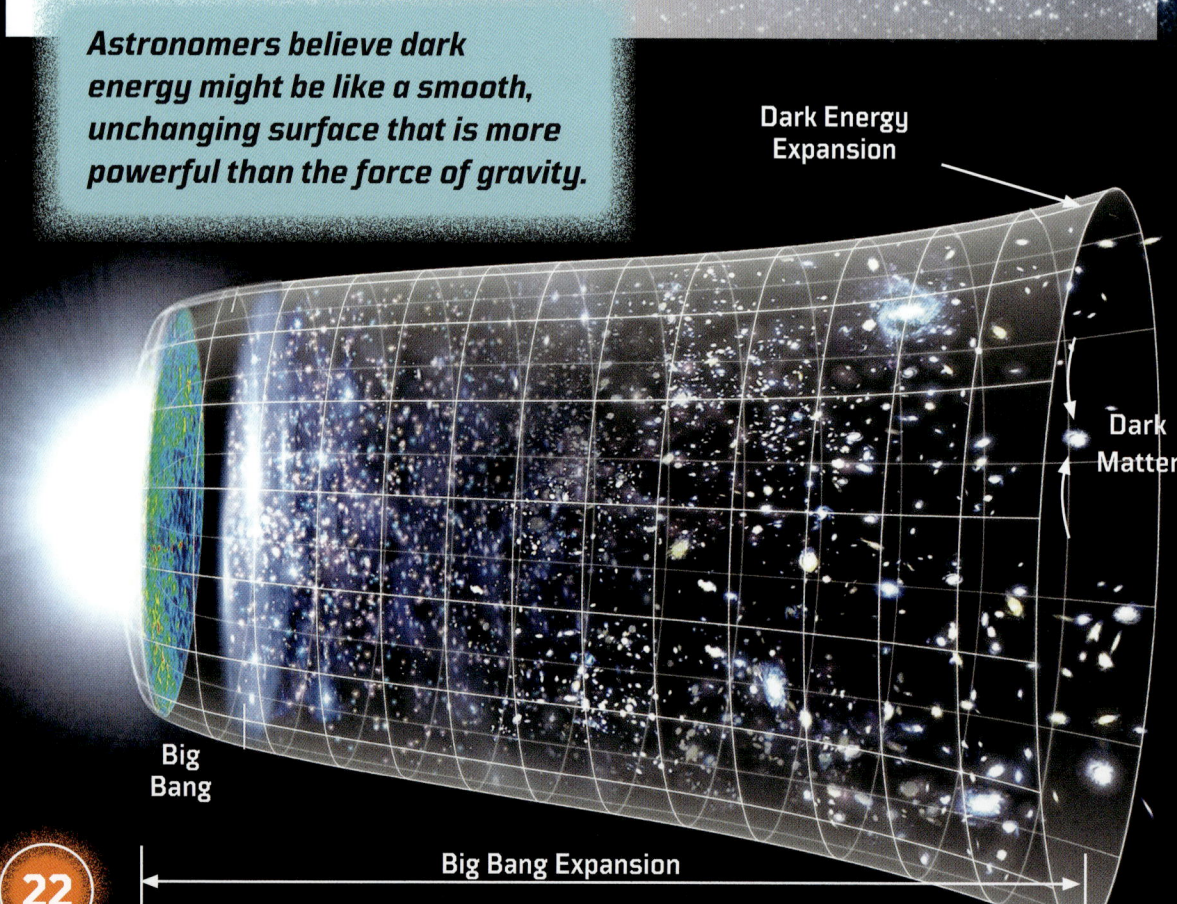

Dark Energy Expansion

Dark Matter

Big Bang

Big Bang Expansion

22

Scientists know that some kind of material exists in the space between the stars because of **gravitational lensing**. This is the distorting of light by gravity. All matter can act like a magnifying glass, bending light from bodies in deep outer space. Using space telescopes, scientists have seen dark matter bend light traveling toward Earth.

Ghost of a Galaxy

What makes up the remaining 70 percent of the universe? Scientists believe it is a force that repels gravity called dark energy. Dark energy is the reason that our universe is expanding.

There is still much to learn about dark energy and dark matter. In March 2018, for example, the HST discovered a "ghost" galaxy. Dark matter holds ordinary matter such as stars and gas together in galaxies. This ghost galaxy is missing not only stars, but is also missing dark matter. To date, no one is sure what the galaxy is made of.

NASA is building a space telescope scheduled to launch in the mid-2020s. The Wide Field Infrared Survey Telescope (WFIRST) will provide the largest pictures of the universe ever seen. WFIRST will measure the effects of dark matter and dark energy on the arrangement of galaxies in the universe. Scientists hope the mission will provide answers to some of the mysteries behind these invisible pieces of the puzzle that is our universe.

The arc-like shape of some distant galaxies is caused by light being bent by gravity in space.

CHAPTER 4

Humans in Outer Space?

Humans have traveled to the Moon, but flying farther into space is too expensive to attempt. When humans take that first step, they will begin with the vehicle that has enabled all space travel so far—the rocket.

Step by Step

More than 100 years ago, U.S. scientist Robert Goddard received his first two patents for rocket technology. In 1919, Goddard wrote a paper arguing that rockets could in theory be used to carry objects as far as the Moon. The press poked fun at his claims. In 1969, as U.S. astronauts made their historic journey to the Moon, *The New York Times* published an apology to him.

Technology continues to take rocket science to the extreme. NASA's space shuttle became the first reusable crewed spacecraft when it was launched in 1981. It could reach speeds close to 18,000 miles per hour (29,000 kph) after liftoff and landed back on Earth like an airplane.

Robert Goddard tows a rocket to a test launch. In 1926, his first rocket rose 41 feet (12.5 m) off the ground.

New Engines

Rockets need to be as strong but as light as possible to reduce the amount of fuel necessary to reach orbit. For engines that are only used in space, such as thrusters for probes, switching resources could be a game changer. Researchers at the University of Michigan are working together with NASA and the U.S. Air Force to develop a new Hall thruster. This engine uses a stream of **ions**, or electrically charged particles, to propel a spacecraft. French scientists are also working on a Hall thruster. Their research could allow space travel using 100 million times less fuel than regular rockets. However, the lifespan of a Hall thruster is only 10,000 hours. That is five times less than is needed for space exploration. Researchers hope to increase that lifespan.

This artist's impression shows NASA's latest rocket, the Space Launch System (SLS).

False Start?

In May 2018, researchers at NASA's Eagleworks advanced-propulsion lab tested technology they hope might one day take humans to Mars in just 70 days. The propulsion engine, which is known as EmDrive, generates thrust by bouncing **microwaves**, which are a form of **electromagnetic** energy, inside a cone-shaped chamber. It has the great advantage of needing no fuel. However, the test was a disappointment. Although some thrust was produced, researchers realized it was not coming from the engine itself. It came instead from an outside source, such as Earth's **magnetic field**. The researchers plan to build a shield to insulate the engine against the effects of magnetism so they can run the tests again.

The Moon and Beyond

NASA's Exploration Mission-1 (EM-1) is the first in a series of missions, each using previously untried technology, that will eventually take humans back to the Moon and beyond. EM-1 will test NASA's deep-space explorations systems, including the Orion spacecraft, the SLS rocket, and the ground systems at Kennedy Space Center in Cape Canaveral, Florida. The project was originally set for launch in 2018 but was then delayed until 2020.

The uncrewed flight will last around three weeks. Orion will stay in space longer than any other spacecraft built to accommodate humans without docking to a space station. Orion will fly to the Moon in just a couple of days. It will then use the gravity of the Moon to shoot into orbit about 43,500 miles (70,000 km) on the other side of the Moon. It will stay in position for around six days, collecting data and giving controllers a chance to see how all of the systems are working.

A Test Mission

Orion will travel around the Moon in a reverse direction from that in which the Moon travels around Earth. On its return trip, Orion will use the precise firing of an engine and the effect of the Moon's gravity in order to accelerate back toward Earth at speeds faster than ever achieved by crewed spacecraft before. Higher speeds will mean higher temperatures when reentering Earth's atmosphere. The mission will test Orion's ability to handle this extreme heat.

Orion is a test vehicle for future crewed missions to deep space.

The Next Step

Assuming that everything works as it is meant to with EM-1, the next step will be Exploration Mission-2 (EM-2). This will be a flight with a crew aboard. All systems will be tested with humans onboard, and the SLS will be reconfigured to carry more cargo in order to support them. If EM-2 is successful, final adjustments will be made to make the SLS and Orion ready for another flight, to dock with a Lunar Orbital Platform-Gateway.

MISSION: Space Science

Construction of EM-2, the next step in sending crewed spacecraft into space, has already begun. It is scheduled to launch in 2023. Such missions are vital for NASA to develop new techniques and apply innovative problem-solving in preparation for longer-duration missions far from Earth.

Astronauts explore the rocky surface of an asteroid in this NASA artwork.

Gateway to Space

The Lunar Orbital Platform-Gateway is a **spaceport**, which is a type of spacecraft where other spacecraft can dock. NASA plans to build this platform sometime in the early 2020s. This space gateway will orbit the Moon. The platform will be made up of several elements, including power and propulsion, and space for living. The pieces of the gateway will be carried into space by the SLS or on **commercial** rockets. The gateway will be assembled in space.

Building a Gateway

Solar electric power and propulsion will be used to keep the platform in orbit, or allow it to be steered into another position in orbit. By 2023, it is planned that the gateway will include living quarters for astronauts and a **logistics** center to oversee such things as communication and ventilation systems. An airlock will allow astronauts to make spacewalks outside of the platform, such as for maintenance. The gateway will allow astronauts to explore the Moon and its resources in greater depth than ever.

Spacecraft will dock onto the platform in the same way space shuttles docked onto the ISS.

The platform will also provide a base for ongoing deep-space research and study. It will become a stepping stone as we inch closer to a human journey to Mars.

Building Prototypes

Six companies were chosen in 2016 to develop prototypes for **habitats**, or living spaces. Bigelow Aerospace is working on XBASE, a small habitat and test platform for deep-space hardware. It will use lessons learned from the Bigelow Expandable Activity **Module** (BEAM). BEAM is an inflatable module inflated with a pressurization system. It was tested on the ISS in 2016 to see how it compares with traditional aluminum modules. Inflatable modules are less bulky to transport and could be the most useful and effective habitat for future space exploration.

The ISS is a testing ground for long-term space travel.

YOUR MISSION

At the moment, planning for deep-space exploration is at an early stage. Scientists and engineers are going back to basics. They are looking at new materials and new methods. The idea of an inflatable module is a complete change from normal rigid spacecraft, for example. Think about the problems such as propulsion and living spaces. Are there any ideas you think scientists should consider—no matter how crazy they might seem?

CHAPTER 5
Ship Shape

Any return trip to Mars is likely to take at least 20 months. It is vital to discover potential health issues that may arise if astronauts spend so long in space. The ISS is a low-gravity environment ideal for testing the technology needed for astronauts to become more **self-sufficient**, or able to support themselves, in space. This technology includes everything from safety equipment to spacesuit design, advanced exercise equipment, and learning to work with robots.

In 2018, there were more than 250 experiments in progress on the ISS. One was testing how the **microgravity** of space might affect **microbes** in astronauts' stomachs. Another was collecting data on crew members' exposure to **radiation**, which is higher in space than on Earth. Another concern is the effect of space flight on bone quality. A new type of bone scan was being tested on the ISS. Scientists will use it to identify early changes in bone health and strength.

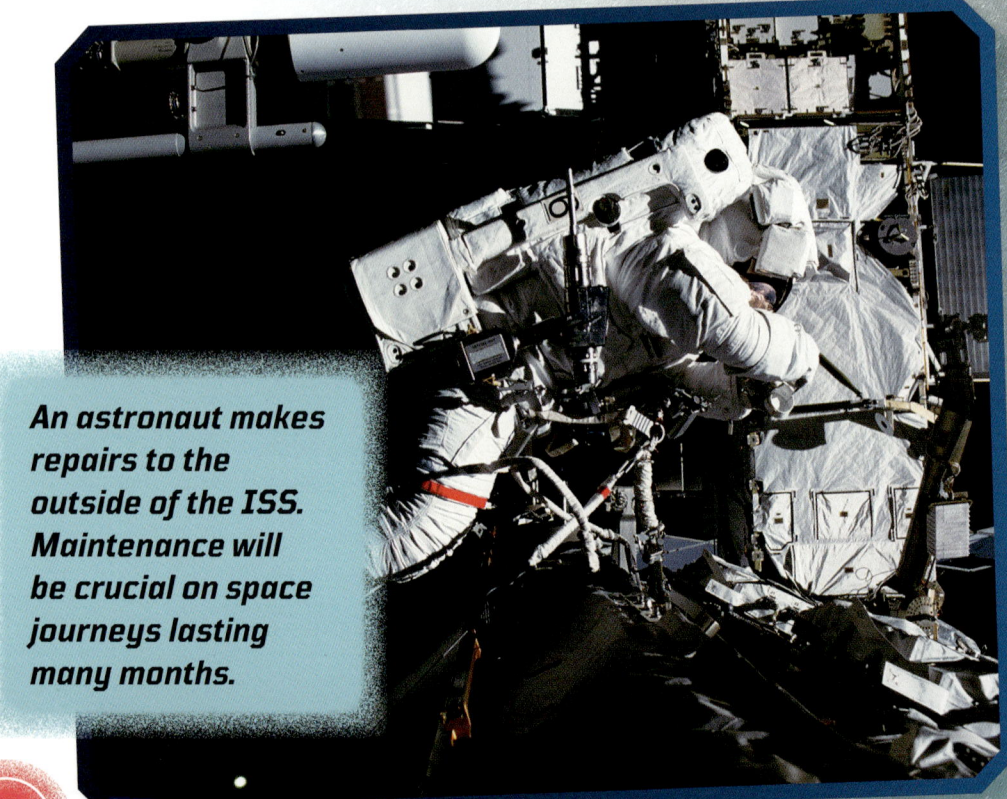

An astronaut makes repairs to the outside of the ISS. Maintenance will be crucial on space journeys lasting many months.

Monitoring Health

Studies on astronauts in space and after their return to Earth are revealing possible ways to reduce health issues. A person's biological clock changes during long periods in space. Researchers are testing the effects of not living in a normal 24-hour cycle of daylight and darkness. They are also looking at the effects that reduced physical activity and living in an artificial environment have on normal body rhythms. Understanding how these influences affect humans in space will help improve performance and health for future astronauts.

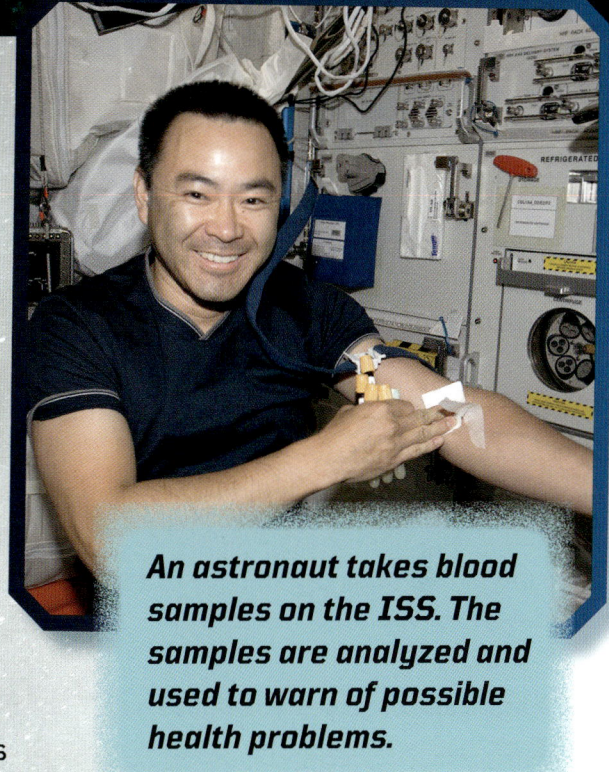

An astronaut takes blood samples on the ISS. The samples are analyzed and used to warn of possible health problems.

Printing in Space

Beyond medical research, current space experiments include such things as creating three-dimensional (3-D) printed parts from plastic. The Additive Manufacturing Facility on the ISS is testing how made-in-space (MIS) printed objects compare with those made on Earth. You never know when an astronaut on the way to Mars might need to print off a precisely shaped plastic switch for a vital piece of equipment!

MISSION: Space Science

Canadian scientists from the University of Saskatchewan are developing a new, lightweight scanner to monitor the health of astronauts during space missions. The device will be strapped to the wearer's ankle. It will check that bone and muscle do not deteriorate during long trips in space. The device should be onboard the ISS by the early 2020s.

A-Roving We Will Go

Whether on the Moon or on Mars, exploring new environments is the perfect job for a rover. Rovers travel across rocky surfaces, and operate in extreme conditions, such as storms that whip up dust from the surface of Mars. They record specific scientific data by testing soils and rocks. So far, three generations of rovers have explored Mars. Each generation has been more sophisticated than the last.

The First Rovers

In 1996, Sojourner traveled about 330 feet (100 m) across the surface of Mars at a maximum speed of 0.4 inch (1 cm) per second. In fewer than three months, Sojourner sent more than 500 images back to Earth and collected chemical data from more than a dozen different locations.

The rovers Spirit and Opportunity arrived almost together on Mars in 2004. They explored two locations on opposite sides of the planet. The rovers were designed to operate for 90 days. Instead, Spirit continued to operate until 2010, and Opportunity was still operating in 2018 and sending data back to Earth. The third generation of Mars rovers saw Curiosity set down in a depression called the Gale Crater in 2012. It found evidence that the ancient Martian environment was once home to water and could have supported life.

Rovers such as Curiosity have to be sturdy to cope with the rocky surface on Mars.

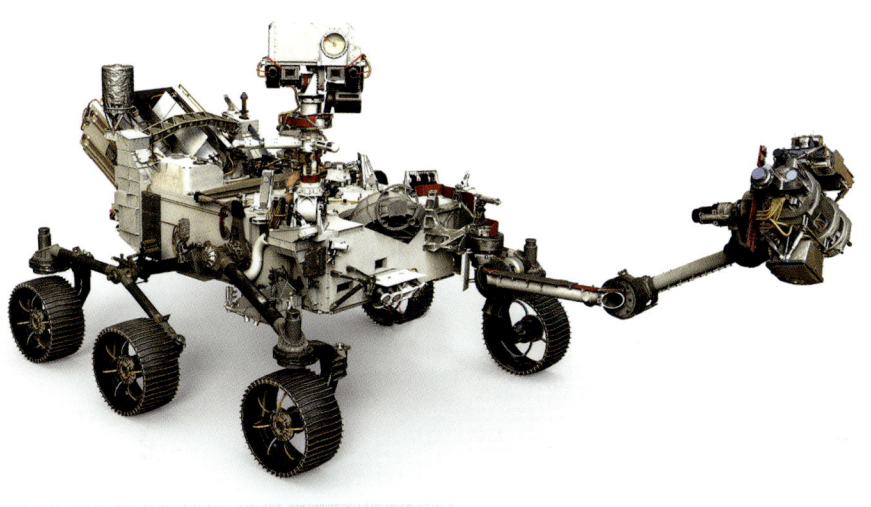

The Mars 2020 rover will carry 23 cameras that can take a range of images, such as microscopic close-ups.

Next Generation

The fourth generation of rover will land on Mars in 2020. It will look for signs of the ancient environment, including **bacteria**, a type of tiny, simple organism, that would show life once existed on Mars. The car-sized rover will also gather data for future human visits, such as finding landing sites and looking for water.

In order to accomplish this, the Mars 2020 rover will carry many special tools to analyze conditions on the planet. It will have a laser to look for chemicals that might suggest life once existed there. A drill will take samples of rock. Other instruments will measure the temperature on the surface, and the speed and direction of the wind. They will also detect any moisture in the air.

Ground-penetrating radar (GPR) will be used to give a more detailed picture of the geological structure that lies beneath the planet's surface. MOXIE, the Mars Oxygen **In-Situ** Resource Utilization Experiment, will practice manufacturing oxygen using the carbon dioxide in the Martian atmosphere.

A 100 Year Starship?

Many ideas about space begin as **science fiction**, which is the creation of imaginary worlds. Writers, artists, and filmmakers imagine worlds that are often based in the future and full of advanced technology. Some of their ideas are unrealistic, such as **teleportation**. This involves sending people instantly through space to appear in a new location. However, other science fiction ideas have inspired scientists to wonder what might be possible. One of these ideas is the creation of a **starship**, a spacecraft that travels between stars.

Spaceship for a Century

In 2011, NASA's 100 Year Starship (100YSS) project began to research a journey between stars to be made in the 2100s. NASA funded a $1 million, year-long 100 Year Starship Study. NASA hoped the study would lead to the development of new kinds of technology that would enable the development of interstellar travel beyond our Solar System. Today, the 100YSS is run by a private company. It has a long-term goal of achieving human interstellar travel.

Will the kinds of spacecraft created for science fiction inspire the next generation of real space vehicles?

No one knows what shape interstellar spacecraft might be. For now, artists use their imaginations.

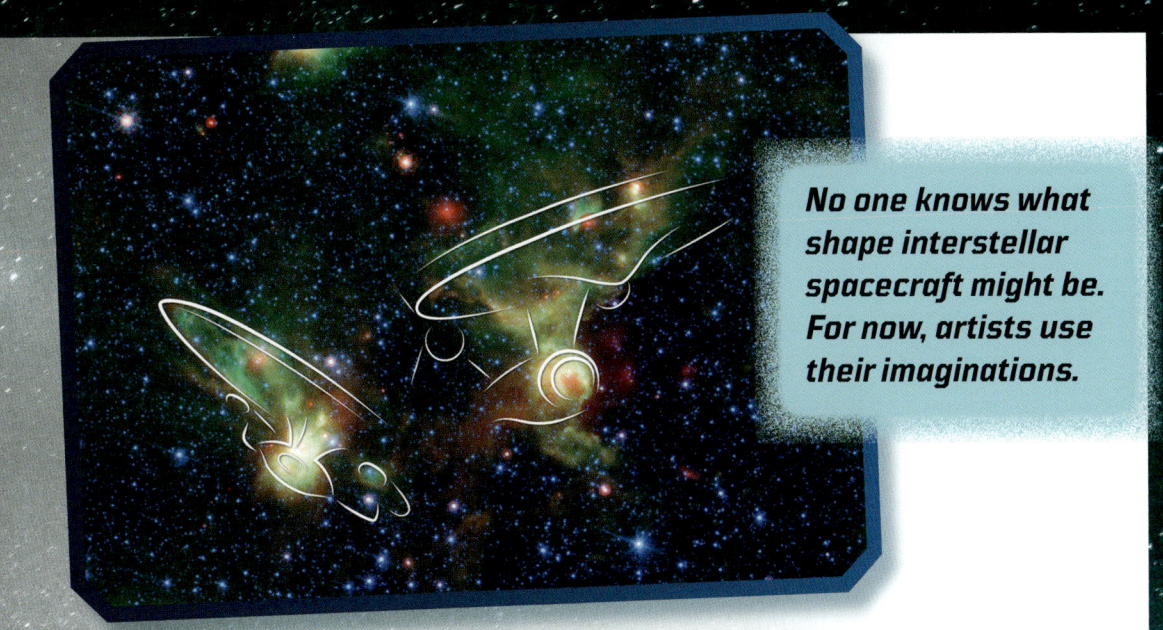

Building a Starship

Starships often appear in science fiction movies such as *Star Wars*. In fact, their design raises many questions. A starship might not resemble an airplane or a rocket, for example. There is no air in space, so a starship might not need to be **aerodynamic**, which is the quality of being able to slide through the air with little resistance.

The Tau Zero Foundation was the brainchild of former NASA engineer Marc Millis. Millis founded Tau Zero as a place for thinking about the long-term future of space exploration. The foundation focuses on interstellar research and education. It looks at emerging possibilities that could change our future. This includes investigating ideas about space stations to allow humans to live in space and faster-than-light flight.

YOUR MISSION

Building a starship that will take 100 years to complete is a very long-term project. How would you encourage people to **invest** in, or put their money into, something that will not be finished until after they are dead? Think about what sort of arguments you would use to convince someone the project is necessary, and what benefits it will eventually bring.

CHAPTER 6
What's Next?

In April 2018, NASA launched its Transiting Exoplanet Survey Satellite (TESS). Like Kepler, this space observatory is designed to hunt for exoplanets. TESS has a far larger field of vision than Kepler. From its position in orbit, the satellite can see 85 percent of the sky.

Searching for Life

TESS will be watching for phenomena called **transits**. A transit occurs when a planet passes between Earth and its star. The planet's crossing in front of the star causes light from the star to dim in brightness for a while at regular intervals as the planet orbits the star. More than three-quarters of the 3,700 or so exoplanets discovered to date were identified using transits. Kepler found around two-thirds of these known exoplanets. Of the exoplanets discovered so far, most orbit stars located 300–3,000 light-years from Earth. TESS will look at brighter stars that are much closer, at 30–300 light-years away. Scientists hope that this pioneering mission to find worlds beyond our Solar System may discover exoplanets that could support life.

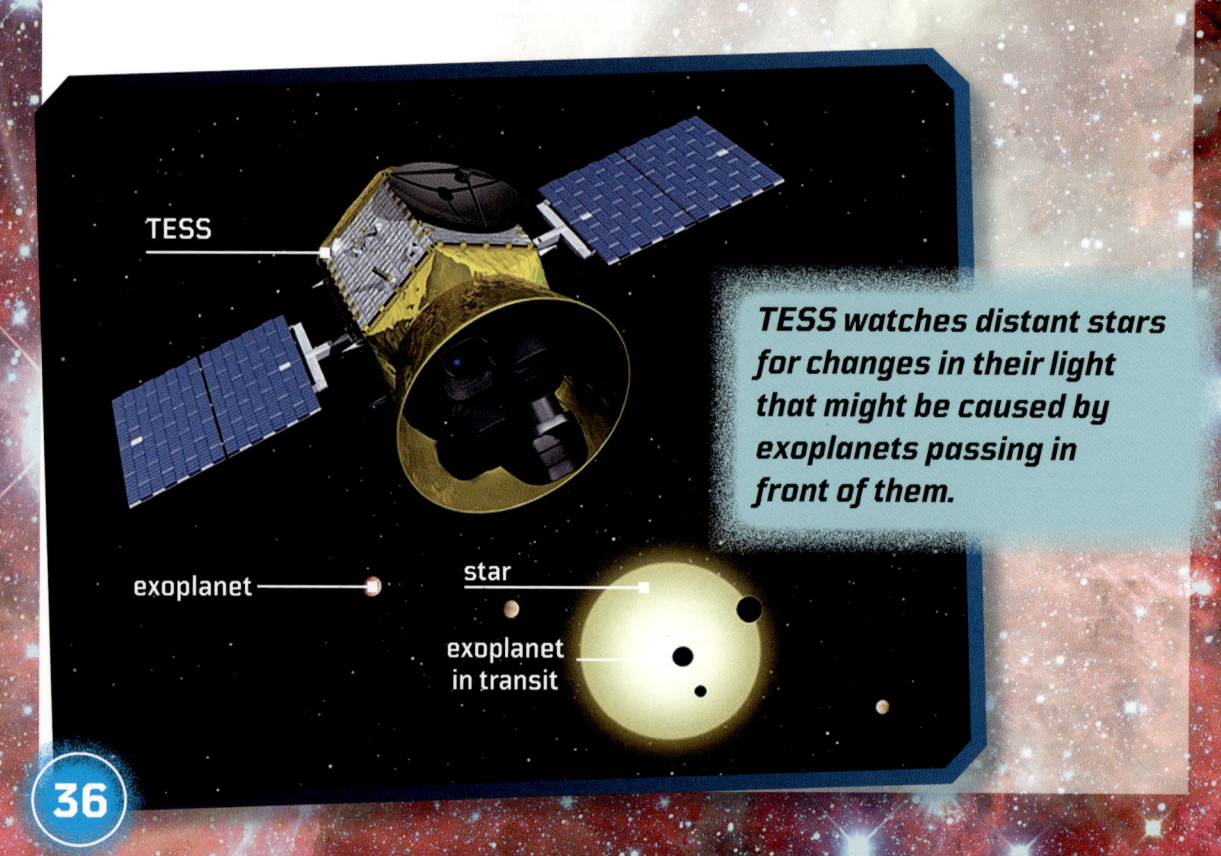

TESS

exoplanet

star

exoplanet in transit

TESS watches distant stars for changes in their light that might be caused by exoplanets passing in front of them.

The James Webb Space Telescope (JWST), due to launch in 2021, will be the most advanced space telescope yet.

MISSION: Space Science

Researchers use **spectroscopy** to determine a planet's mass, density, and atmosphere. Water and other clues in its atmosphere point to whether the planet is capable of supporting life.

The Mission Begins

After settling into orbit and being thoroughly tested, TESS began transmitting its first scientific data back to Earth in August 2018. It will continue to download data to Earth once every orbit, or every 13.5 days. The data will be reviewed by astronomers. More than a dozen universities, research institutes, and observatories around the world are part of the TESS mission.

A New Telescope

The JWST is planned to be a powerful and complex infrared observatory. Its cutting-edge technology has caused numerous delays in building the telescope. The technology has to be tested and fine-tuned before it goes into orbit. JWST is the result of collaboration between three main agencies. These are NASA, the European Space Agency (ESA), and the Canadian Space Agency (CSA). The telescope will help solve some of the mysteries of our Solar System and look for others. It will also probe the origins of our universe and our place in it. It is planned that JWST will take some of the exoplanets discovered by TESS and examine their atmospheres.

Decades of Discovery

In 2020, the U.S. National Academy of Sciences (NAS) is due to publish the Astro2020 **Decadal** Survey. It is one of a series of regular ten-year surveys of **astronomy** and astrophysics. The survey has two main roles. It reviews our current knowledge of astronomy and outlines missions and priorities for NASA for the next 10 years. The Astro2020 Decadal Survey will ask big questions. How did the universe begin and how will it end? What is the origin of the universe's structure of galaxies, stars, and planets? Are we alone? The focus will be on developing probes to explore outer space and start the search for answers to these questions.

2010 Decadal Survey

The last decadal survey was published in 2010. Since then, the way scientists view the universe has changed dramatically. More than 3,400 exoplanets have been discovered orbiting distant stars. Black holes are now known to be present at the center of most galaxies, including the Milky Way. The age, size, and shape of the universe have been mapped based on the ancient radiation left over by the Big Bang. Scientists have also learned that most of the matter in the universe is dark and invisible, and that the universe is expanding, or getting bigger.

The Sombrero Galaxy is 28 million light-years away. At its heart is a black hole 1 billion times more massive than the Sun.

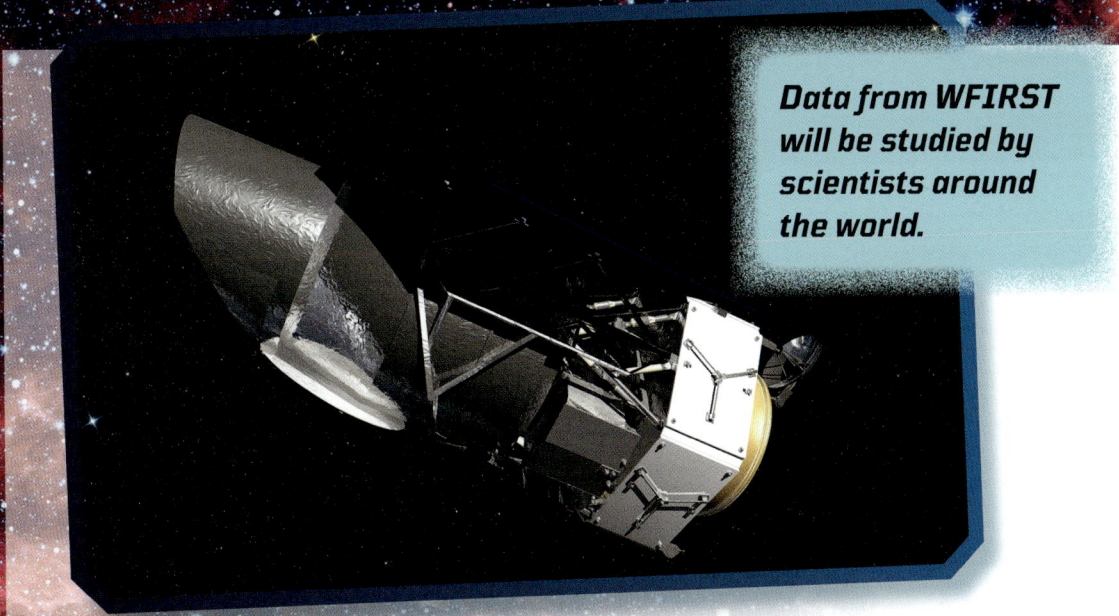

Data from WFIRST will be studied by scientists around the world.

Future Missions

The 2010 decadal survey suggested that the top priority for space research was the construction of the Wide Field Infrared Survey Telescope (WFIRST). This space telescope was intended to unravel the secrets of dark energy and dark matter. NASA began building the telescope in February 2016.

NASA also runs a program called Small Explorers (SMEX). It promotes cheaper missions to investigate specific subjects raised by the decadal survey. One mission, the Imaging X-ray Polarimetry Explorer (IXPE), will explore different forms of light in space to help us understand how X-rays are produced by objects such as black holes or **neutron stars**, which are dense, collapsed stars. Another mission will investigate the origins of the gas between stars in the Milky Way. The space observatory GUSTO will measure the amount of gas in space beyond Earth's atmosphere.

YOUR MISSION

Why not carry out your own decadal survey? From what you have read in this book, what would you most like to find out about space during the next 10 years? Give reasons for your choices.

Look Out!

The 2010 Decadal Survey suggested that NASA construct four telescopes. One was the Large Ultraviolet, Optical, and Infrared Observatory (LUVOIR). It would be a space observatory that would study the different wavelengths of light mentioned in its name. It would use them to study everything from the evolution of galaxies to the formation of stars, planets, and solar systems. Another planned telescope was Lynx, a next-generation X-ray observatory. Lynx would allow astrophysicists to see the invisible spaces of the universe for the first time. It was hoped that it would reveal the birth of supermassive black holes and provide information about the lifespan of stars.

This poster for LUVOIR shows some of the hexagonal segments that will make up its mirror.

The remaining two telescopes were the Origins Space Telescope (OST) and the Habitable Exoplanet Observatory (HabEx), which would study planetary systems around stars that resemble our Sun. These missions were planned to work in related ways to answer the question of whether there is life elsewhere in the universe. They would find exoplanets and study the chances of life on each.

Reducing Costs

NASA scientists began planning to build the telescopes. However, in 2018, NASA became concerned about the costs of the telescopes. It instructed its teams to go back to their plans and come up with cheaper versions of the missions.

The original design for LUVOIR had a mirror measuring about 49 feet (15 m) in diameter. The mirror was made up of adjustable **segments**, or parts, that would unfold once the observatory reached its orbit in space. Motors would adjust the mirror to capture light from faint, distant objects. The new design of the observatory is known as LUVOIR-B. It has the same basic segmented mirror as the original, but the mirror will be around 50 percent smaller.

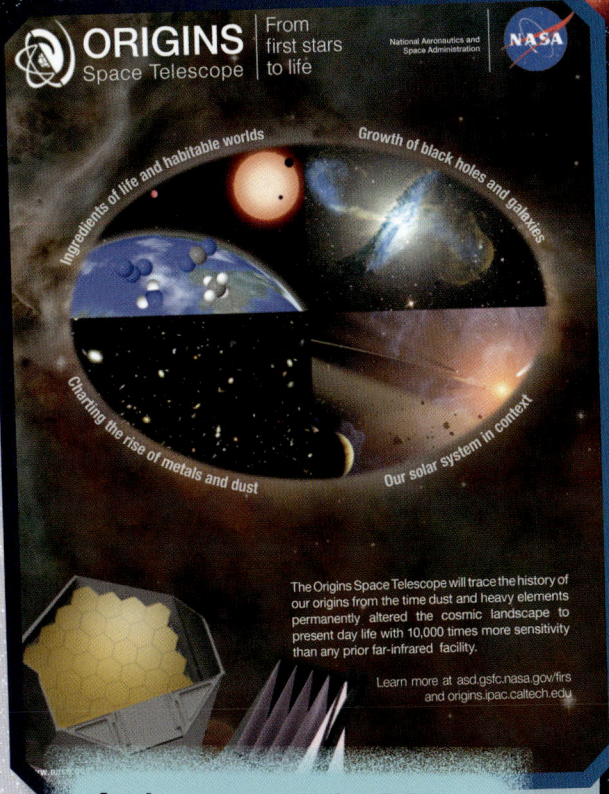

At the moment, the OST only exists on paper. It remains to be seen if it is ever built.

Uncertain Future

Engineers also came up with less costly versions of Lynx, the OST, and HabEx, but eight years after the 2010 decadal survey, all four telescopes remained in the planning stages. All four will have to resubmit their plans and new costs to the 2020 Decadal Survey. Whether the projects continue or not will remain uncertain. The new survey may decide to change the priorities for space research for the 2020s.

All Passengers Aboard!

Your space flight is ready for takeoff—well, almost ready. NASA is looking at ways to involve private businesses in the funding of the ISS. Meanwhile, private companies are competing to be the first to take the paying public for a flight into space.

A Commercial Space

SpaceX was founded in 2002 by the businessman Elon Musk. The company aims to develop technology that will eventually help people live in space. It has already taken a number of significant steps. It has developed spacecraft to carry food, equipment, and astronauts to the ISS on behalf of NASA. SpaceX continues to develop more powerful rockets, such as the Falcon Heavy. In 2018, it signed up Japanese billionaire Yusaku Maezawa as its first space tourist. He will orbit the Moon in 2023.

SpaceX is not the only company vying for space travel contracts. Boeing is collaborating with NASA to develop crew transportation. The Starliner spacecraft is designed to carry seven passengers or a mix of crew and cargo. It can be reused up to 10 times before it needs servicing and repair work.

Dragon made its first trip to resupply the ISS in 2012. It was contracted to visit 26 more times before 2024.

Virgin designed SpaceShipTwo (SS2) to carry space tourists to the edge of the atmosphere.

Crewed Flights

In August 2018, NASA announced crew assignments for the first major flights of both SpaceX and Boeing's spacecraft for carrying crew into space. These test crews will be the first passengers to ride on the respective spacecraft. It is their task to see if the spacecraft are ready to make regular trips to the ISS. The first test flights for both spacecraft were scheduled for 2019. Both companies were required to do an uncrewed test flight followed by a crewed flight. Only if these test flights are successful can the spacecraft be cleared to carry out routine flights to and from the ISS.

Going Public

Virgin Galactic, the world's first commercial spaceline, was founded by the British businessman Sir Richard Branson. Its mission is to open access to space, to change the world for good. The company's SpaceShipTwo consists of a specially built carrier aircraft, WhiteKnightTwo, and a spaceship. VSS Unity is the first Virgin Galactic spaceship. It completed its first supersonic, rocket-powered flight safely in April 2018. That year, there were more customers who had paid to reserve places to fly on SpaceShipTwo than the number of astronauts who have ever been to space in the past.

ACTIVITY
Your Space Science Mission

A lander is a probe that descends from an orbiting spacecraft to the surface of a moon or another planet. Landers make soft landings to protect their instruments, which sometimes include rovers. Landers are important in deep-space research because they gather data about a moon or planet's environment. They are the first stage of onsite exploration.

Building a deep-space lander involves a lot of planning. The lander's protective shell protects the rover from the forces of impact. It has to be lightweight but super strong, and able to withstand environmental dangers. It also has to be foolproof. If the lander fails to open after reaching the surface, the rover will not be able to leave. The whole mission will be a failure.

Research the best materials and equipment for a lander that is suitable for Mars.

Planning Your Mission

1. Decide on your goals.
What do you want to learn about Mars? If you are looking for evidence that the planet once had water on its surface, it might be most useful to explore low regions that might be ancient lake beds. If you are looking for minerals, you might need a drill to take samples from the rocks.

2. Research the challenges.
Mars is cold, lifeless, and very windy. Winds fill the sky with dust and sand. There is more radiation than on Earth. Research different materials to decide what is best to protect your sensitive instruments. You could start here: technology.grc.nasa.gov.

3. Research other landers.
Three generations of landers have explored Mars. What methods were used to protect the landers from impact? What options were used to open the landers to release the rovers? What materials were used to build the spacecraft? What equipment was onboard? What worked well, and what failed?

4. Figure out what you will need.
Put together a brief paper that outlines the equipment and materials you need for your mission.

5. Design your lander.
Draw a sketch of what your lander might look like. Remember to include protection for the landing on Mars, and a method for ensuring the lander is upright. Show how the lander will open to release the rover.

6. Collaborate!
Once you have some ideas jotted down, share them with a friend. See if they can come up with suggestions and new ideas to add to yours.

Glossary

Please note: Some **bold-faced** words are defined where they appear in the book.

antennae Devices for detecting radio signals
aperture An opening in a lens through which light passes
asteroids Rocky bodies that orbit the Sun
astronomy The study of space and the universe
astrophysicists Scientists who study bodies in space
atoms The smallest particles of an element that can exist
Big Bang The theory that the universe began with a huge explosion
biotechnology The use of biological materials and processes in industry
comets Bodies made of ice and dust that travel around the Sun
commercial Operated as a business for profit
dark energy A form of energy that acts in the opposite way to dark matter, by pushing the universe apart
dwarf planet A small body that orbits a star
electromagnetic Related to electrical or magnetic waves traveling in space
evolving Becoming more advanced
galaxies Massive collections of gas, dust, stars, and planets
geological Related to the study of rocks
gravity A force that attracts all objects toward one another
infrared A type of radiation that is invisible to the human eye
in-situ In its original place
laser A highly focused beam of light
logistics The organization of complex operations
magnetic field A region with a magnetic charge
mass The amount of matter in an object
microbes Tiny organisms
microgravity Very weak gravity
module A self-contained part of a spacecraft
observatories Buildings or spacecraft designed for looking at space
optical Related to vision
phenomena Events that can be observed
planets Bodies in space that orbit stars
prototype A trial version of an invention
radiation The giving off of energy in the form of light or heat
remotely From a distance
robotic Able to perform mechanical tasks based on programmed instructions
satellites Natural or artificial objects that orbit a planet or star
sensor A device that detects something
solar system A group of planets that orbit a star
spectrometers Devices used to measure light
spectroscopy Using light to study materials
telescopes Instruments that gather information about distant objects
theories Explanations of phenomena based on general ideas
transits Occasions when one body crosses in front of another
X-rays Invisible waves of electromagnetic energy

Learning More

Books

Abbott, Simon. *100 Questions about Outer Space*. Peter Pauper Press, Inc., 2018.

DeCristofano, Carolyn. *Ultimate Space Atlas* (National Geographic Kids). National Geographic Children's Books, 2017.

Kopp, Megan. *Space Tech: High Tech Space Science* (Techno Planet). Crabtree Publishing Company, 2018.

Rooney, Anne. *Astronomers in Action* (Scientists in Action). Crabtree Publishing Company, 2018.

Websites

Discover more about how radio astronomy works at:
http://encyclopedia.kids.net.au/page/ra/Radio_astronomy

To find out more about telescopes, log on at:
https://www.universetoday.com/14424/telescopes

Want to find out more about the HST? Try this site:
www.nasa.gov/mission_pages/hubble/story/the_story.html

If you want to find out more about gravitational waves, watch an awesome explanation here:
youtu.be/4GbWfNHtHRg

Index

ALMA (telescope) 9
asteroids 5, 12, 13
astronauts 6, 27, 28, 29, 30–31, 42, 43
atmosphere 4, 10

Big Bang 20, 38
black holes 18–19, 20, 21, 38, 41

Chandra X-ray Observatory 20, 21
commercial spacecraft 42–43

dark energy 22, 23, 39
dark matter 7, 22, 23, 38, 39
decadal surveys 38, 40, 41
Deep Space Network (DSN) 11

Earth 4, 7, 8–9, 10, 12, 25
energy 7, 12, 20, 22, 23, 39
exoplanets 7, 36, 37, 38
expanding universe 20, 23, 38

FAST (telescope) 9

galaxies 5, 18, 23, 38
gravitational lensing 23
gravitational waves 19, 21
gravity 16, 22, 23, 26, 30

Hubble Space Telescope (HST) 23

infrared light 10, 11
International Space Station (ISS) 15, 29, 30, 31, 42, 43

interstellar space 17, 34, 35, 39

James Webb Space Telescope (JWST) 37
Jupiter 16, 17

Kepler space telescope 11

landers 12, 44–45
life in space 7, 32, 33, 36, 37, 41
light-years 4, 5, 7, 8, 19, 36, 38
living and working in space 28–29, 30–31
LSST (telescope) 9
Lunar Orbital Platform-Gateway 28–29

Mars 6, 8, 13, 25, 29, 30, 32–33, 45
matter 22, 23, 38, 39
microgravity 30
Milky Way 5, 8, 18, 21, 38
Moon 6, 8, 24, 26, 28
moons 16, 17

NASA 10, 11, 16, 20, 23, 25, 27, 28, 34, 36, 37, 39, 41, 42, 43

orbiters 12
Orion spacecraft 26, 27

planets 5, 7, 12, 13, 16–17, 22, 32–33, 36
probes 12–17, 32–33, 38, 44–45

radiation 19, 30, 38
radio waves 8
robotic exploration 13, 14–15
rockets 7, 24–25, 26, 28, 42
rovers 12, 13, 14–15, 32–33

satellites 10, 36–37, 42
Saturn 16, 17
solar system 5, 12
space shuttles 24, 28
space telescopes 10–11, 23, 37
spacecraft 26–31, 34–35, 42–43
spaceports 28–29
SpaceX 42, 43
stars 4, 5, 7, 10, 11, 18, 20, 22, 36, 41
starships 34–35
storms 16
Sun 5, 17

telescopes 5, 7, 8–11, 23, 37, 39, 40–41
Thirty Meter Telescope (TMT) 9
Transiting Exoplanet Survey Satellite (TESS) 36–37
transits 36

Uranus 17

volcanoes 16

Wide Field Infrared Survey Telescope (WFIRST) 23, 39

X-rays 10, 20, 21, 41

About the Author

Megan Kopp is a children's book writer who lives in the Rocky Mountains. While she enjoys reading and writing about space science, she has her feet firmly planted on the ground!